HOLLY LISLE

The Professional Plot Outline

Mini-Course

Published by Holly Lisle

Print ISBN: 978-1468025859

Cover Design: Holly Lisle

Cover Art: (the penguin) Jan Martin Will / Bigstock.com

Holly's Author Photo: © Holly Lisle

DISCLAIMER AND/OR LEGAL NOTICES:
The information in this course has been built from my life and experiences, and it is what works for me. While I have made every effort to translate the decidedly quirky workings of one human mind into a process that will be applicable and accessible to other human minds, I cannot guarantee that this course will work for you, or that my processes will be applicable to your needs and purposes. Nor can I guarantee your success. This course is not intended as a source of legal, accounting, medical or other advice, and is written for information purposes only. While every attempt has been made to verify the information in this course, mistakes happen, and I make them. I will not assume responsibility for errors, inaccuracies, or omissions. I reserve the right to alter and update this course as my processes change, as I learn new things, and as I improve existing methods.

My Students Say:

"I JUST SIGNED up for your 'Create Your Professional Plot Outline' mini-course. Wow! Just utterly WOW! From the get-go, you've helped me figure out what's been holding me up in the story I've been trying to write for two years now! After several other courses, books and suggestions, I'd begun to think maybe I'd just ditch the story. Maybe there wasn't really enough substance to hold a reader (or this writer) past the first few chapters. Or maybe, much as it hurt to say it, maybe I just didn't have it in me.

"Exercise One gave me some reflection on my main character, but Exercise Two? Simply reading the exercise gave me that elusive "A-HA! That's the problem" moment I've been needing ever since I stalled in chapter six (more than a year ago). You've helped me see where and how I was sabotaging the story (overcomplication of plot and too many main protagonists), and you did so in an easy, practical way.

"I can't wait to actually DO the exercise... so I'm off to do that right now, but I had to say thanks first! I'm so excited, I plan to work late into the night, restructuring the story to go where it really wanted to be heading in the first place.

"Thank you so much for offering this course, and for your support of would-be novelists like myself.

"Looking forward to your other classes as well!"

Best regards,
Alice

"A YEAR AGO I decided to become a writer. Since then I have purchased books and taken on-line courses. I recently completed one book, have 2 in process, and a series in the works.

"After reading and taking copious notes on 15-20 books about writing, I came across Holly Lisle while doing internet searches. I have found her course material to be very direct and useful. Most other courses tend to be vague and preachy. Holly has led me to using Scrivener, to step-by-step approaches, and a nitty-gritty, focused approach to working through revisions. I haven't had to leave my home to develop quickly as an author.

"The **Create A Plot Clinic** and **Plot-Outline Mini-Course** are especially helpful. The plot is at the center of the novel. It is the backbone where the meat can hang off of as your novel takes shape.

"Holly is wacky and fun, but underneath, she teaches a direct approach that can cut years off of the time it takes to become a serious, production oriented novelist."

Joe Carlin—Cary, NC

"HOLLY LISLE is one of the rare writers who can not only write, but also teach others how to write. She is able to take the mystery out of plotting, giving step-by-step instruction that will enable you to plot your novels with the confidence of a master.

"In her own inimitable style, Holly tells you like it is, and she should know—she's authored more than thirty published novels. Regardless of your skill level, you will most definitely come away from Holly's course knowing exactly what to do and how to do it."

Laurel—Wilmington, Delaware

"I TOOK THE **Plot Mini-Course** *a few years ago. It was my first experience of Holly's method, and I immediately fell in love with her no-nonsense, hands-on teaching style.*

"And it worked like magic, too: I had never even imagined plotting like this, and was blown away with the wonderful, fun, and devilishly effective technique taught in the course.

"Now, several clinics, quite a few workshops, two big courses, a revision, and a novel and a half later, I'm ever so grateful for that one mini-course that introduced me to a whole new writing world."

Ivye—Italy

STOP! You Get Worksheets, Too!

This course includes downloadable, printable worksheets that support Section II lessons.

Before you start, create your free account on my site and get your PDF worksheets.

http://HowToThinkSideways.com/join-us

You'll receive an email with your login information, so make sure before you submit your information that you do not have any typos or errors in your e-mail address.

Some free email providers, among them AOL, Hotmail, and Yahoo mail, frequently delete autogenerated emails rather than delivering them.

If you use one of these addresses to create your account, be aware that you may not receive your login email, and the only solution is to use a different email provider and create a new account with a different user name.

If you require free email, my students have had good delivery results with Gmail.

You may also want to explore other free email alternatives:

http://www.fepg.net/emailtypes.html

Once you've registered and logged in, click the link below to go to your Plot Outline downloads page:

http://howtothinksideways.com/plot-outline-course

This page will not work unless you are logged in.

When you register and login, you will find your worksheets download page along with an invitation to join my private Writers' Bootcamps. Classroom membership is not a course requirement, and the course stands complete on its own.

"May I print out the worksheets so everyone in my writer's group can do the exercises together?"

Yes, you may.

If you'd rather not foot the whole bill for paper and printer toner every week, though, you can suggest each member get their own copy of the ebook and the free worksheets, and bring their worksheets with them to the meeting.

Introduction:
What We're Doing Here

No one ever says, "You cannot teach someone to be a surgeon. He has to be *born* a surgeon."

How many surgeons are you willing to go to who haven't been *taught* the science of surgery? None? Me, either.

But I've heard countless people, including writers who damn well ought to know better, saying, "You can't teach someone to be a writer. He has to be *born* a writer."

What these writers mean is that *they* can't teach someone to be a writer. Which is what they ought to say, only I guess it's more fun to pretend that writing is some mysterious gift of the gods, sprinkled down on the heads of the exalted few.

It's not. Writing is not magic, it's not some ephemeral gift of an invisible muse, and it's not something people are just born with.

Writing is a skill. Like surgery.

If a surgeon who understands what he's doing and why he does it can teach a fellow human being to repair a man's shredded arteries, replace his heart or his kidney, or remove a tumor from his brain in time to save his life, a writer who understands what

1

she's doing and why she does it can teach a fellow human being how to tell a story in a coherent, interesting fashion.

So that's what you and I are doing here. I know something cool, which is how to put a story together in a way that makes people want to read it all the way to the end, and I'm going to teach you how to do that.

While I'm doing that, you're going to discover that you CAN learn this skill idiots claim cannot be taught.

And if you like doing it enough, I have other courses available that offer *in-depth* training on everything from creating interesting characters, cultures, languages and worlds, to plotting and writing page-turning scenes, to writing and revising novels and building your career as a full-time writer.

And that's my Evil Plan. I'm going to cleverly show you that I can teach you to do something well that you'll love to do...

...So you'll buy my other courses and learn the rest of the skills required to make a career writing fiction...

...So you'll become a full-time novelist yourself, writing fiction joyfully through the rest of your life and creating a steady flow of great books other people will love to read.

Including me, because I gotta tell you, I can't stand most of the inept, sloppy storytelling on the shelves right now. I WANT SOMETHING GOOD TO READ. I'd be thrilled to buy it from you.

If, of course, that's your dream.

Maybe while I'm at it I can convince you that if you like this course, you'll like my novels. Because they're good, and the same brain, and the same offbeat sense of humor, created both.

Or maybe I can do both. You're neck deep in Evil Plans now, Sparky.

So. Wanna learn something really cool?

Holly Lisle

SECTION I

Creating A
Professional Plot Outline

In this workshop you'll develop the basics of a working plot outline, starting with a character-based idea and finishing with a first outline draft that you can use to write your story or book.

Work your way through the initial five mini-chapters in **Section I**, then go to the techniques and processes in the seven lessons in **Section II**. The lessons were designed to be done at a one-per-week pace for folks who work full-time jobs and need to do just a little writing at a time. You may of course work through them at any pace you like.

You can develop an idea from any of a number of directions. Start with:

- a structure
- questions
- a twist
- a character
- worldbuilding,
- or more than a dozen other entry points into your story

For this workshop, I'll demonstrate plot development techniques using an idea drawn from character development.

- **I'll explain the process.**

- **I'll give you a demonstration.**

- **And then you'll you'll do an exercise that will build a part of your plot.**

STEP 1: Figure Out Your Character

- **First, sum up what you know about your character in one short paragraph**

HERE'S MY EXAMPLE:

I like my character Cadence Drake, so I'll use her as the main character in this workshop. From her previous book, **Hunting the Corrigan's Blood**, I know that:

Cadence Drake is a finder of lost things, primarily hired by corporations who can afford her high fees, that she lost her best friend in a firefight, that she has a really cool experimental prototype spaceship for which she does not have legal paperwork, and, though this may or may not be relevant for this book, she has injected herself with a serum that is toxic to the recombinantly-created vampires who have developed a powerful cabal in her universe.

Just rehashing this abbreviated biography has given me some clues to the story I want to write next. And some things I don't want to write, as well.

EXERCISE ONE:

Write your own single paragraph in your writing notebook describing what you know about your main character. Keep it short and focus on the most important things—what he **values**, what he **does**, what he **needs**, what he **wants**, what he **fears**.

[Do the EXERCISE ONE worksheet, then continue.]

STEP 2: Decide On Your Central Idea

- **Determine what you like and don't like about your original summary**

HERE'S MY EXAMPLE:

I don't want to follow up on the vampire thread in this second story; I developed a huge universe for Cady, and I don't want to get bogged down in that one tiny facet of it and have the books stereotyped as vampire books.

I do want to follow up on the death of Badger, Cady's long-time best friend and sometimes lover, who was killed in a firefight.

And I have discovered a device to get me into the story, as well. Cadence doesn't have legal papers for her ship, the Corrigan's Blood, which she acquired when one of her employers tried to kill her in lieu of paying her. The employer ended up dead instead, and Cadence helped herself to his ship. I see the entry point to this story being the fact that if Cady is going to keep this ship - and she IS going to keep this ship - she has to acquire some good fake papers for it. And fast.

EXERCISE TWO:

Select and list below the points you want to pursue, the ideas that you find fascinating and compelling. Three or four items will be enough.

[Do the EXERCISE TWO worksheet, then continue.]

STEP 3: Write Your Opener

HERE'S MY EXAMPLE:

So from the following tiny bit of background,

- best friend & partner dead

- piloting stolen spaceship

- profession is finder of lost things for well-heeled clients

...I have my opening set-up. Cadence is going to go looking for a place to get quality fake papers, and because the rightful owner of the ship is dead under suspicious, even dreadful, circumstances, she has to get the papers from someone not inclined to ask questions. This suggests moving into a risky situation, and I think she'll meet a dangerous but interesting character—one who is willing to give her the papers she wants in exchange for the barter of her services. He'll give her time-limited interim papers, and in exchange she'll find something important of his that has gone missing.

We'll worry about what that is later. For now, I have a solid opening for this new novel that accomplishes the following essential tasks:

- Introduces my main character

- Gives her a motive for moving from a situation of danger into a situation of more danger

- Brings in a second character of less than sterling reputation for the hero to play off

EXERCISE THREE:

Time for you to do the same. Using any ideas you have about your character, put together in the space provided a single paragraph that focuses on the critical parts of your character—what he does, what he needs, and what he fears—that answers the following questions:

- **What is the most difficult thing my character is struggling with right now?**

- **How does that struggle give him one problem he must solve?**

- **Who or what will stand in the way of the solution he seeks?**

[Do the EXERCISE THREE worksheet, then continue.]

Got your opener now? Good. Let's move on to your ending.

STEP 4: Create Your Ending

If your first reaction is, "What am I going to do with an ending when I have only the foggiest idea of my beginning, and none whatsoever of my middle?" don't worry. You aren't going to do a completely written-out chapter. All you're going to do is figure out a basic landing pad for your story.

HERE'S MY EXAMPLE:

In my case, I'll make the following decisions:

- Cadence will live (the survival of the main character is not always a given in my books, and eventually Cadence may make an irreversibly fatal mistake - but not this book)

- She will find what she's been sent to find

- It will not be what she was led to expect, and this surprise will nearly cost her her life, and will prove fatal to at least one person the reader has come to know (though not necessarily to like)

- She will have her reckoning with the man who used her

- Maybe she will get her papers - that I'll decide later.

EXERCISE FOUR:

Go back to your opener and figure out in general terms how you want the story to end.

[Do the first part of the EXERCISE FOUR worksheet, then continue.]

When you have your list, answer the following questions in your notebook:

- **Does your protagonist succeed or fail in gaining the objective you gave him in your opener?**

- **Does your story come to an emotionally satisfying conclusion?**

- **Can you see yourself writing through anywhere from ten pages to seven hundred and being happy to see the story end this way?**

[Do the second part of the EXERCISE FOUR worksheet, then continue.]

STEP 5: Rough In Your Middle

You have your beginning and your ending. Now we need to add some middle, throw in some neat twists and turns, and give you something so great to work on that you'll be excited about sitting down to work on your book every day.

So we're going to build some candy-bar scenes to move you from first word in your story to last.

I've mentioned candy-bar scenes in other articles and workshops. They're my analogy for scenes you can't resist writing —your big set piece scenes. In these scenes, your characters will fight battles, save lives or take them, fall into or out of love, meet their enemies in unexpected places, chase or be chased.

You don't need to work these out in any great detail. A line or two to give you something to shoot for is all you need. Even order doesn't matter at this point - that will come as you start fleshing your story out.

HERE'S MY EXAMPLE:

For example, I know in this story that I'm starting to tell now, I want the following things:

- a great spaceship dogfight

- Cadence meets a potential new partner

- meeting up with Tangerine (a character from **HTCB**)

- run-in with a one of the minions of the stellar-regional underground that ends in a gunfight

- Cadence sides with the underworld against area law enforcement, which is holding whatever she's after

- A recent acquaintance is murdered in terrible circumstances, and law enforcement arrests Cady

- The person she suspects of the murder breaks her out of the jail at great personal risk

And so on . . .

Every scene I jot down spurs ideas for more scenes. As I run with this, I'll put together enough main scenes to peg into my novel, and then start creating transitions and connections to move me from one "candy-bar scene" to the next.

How many is enough? Depends on what you want to write. There's no set number for any project, but you need at least three scenes for all but the shortest short stories, and at least one big scene per chapter for novels. A 125,000 word novel can have thirty or forty chapters (or more) with two or three scenes in each. I use ten pages as my scene-length estimate, and either twenty or thirty pages as my chapter-length estimate, and 230 words as my words-per-page estimate, and work from there.

EXERCISE FIVE

Your turn. With your beginning and your ending in front of you, sketch in between three and sixty one-line scene ideas. (You'll find twenty tools for making this process much, much easier in **Holly Lisle's Create A Plot Clinic**, generally available where you purchased this book.)

I suggest coming up with more than you think you're going to need, because from my own experience over the years, about 20% of your ideas will turn out to be unusably bad.

For this exercise, use index cards, or print out the EXERCISE FIVE plot cards.

STEP 6: Make Everything Add Up

This is the bare bones of the process I use for developing novels. The outline that I get the first time through is subject to revision, cutting, rearranging, and midcourse correction. It's a working document—a tool—and as such it is never really finished.

It is a reflection of where the novel is, and where I think it is going, and I usually abandon it completely three-quarters of the way through my book. But it's always there when I need to rethink something.

It will be there for you, too. A good plot outline can be any dedicated writer's best friend.

So, with the basics out of the way, it's time for Section II, and the lessons.

SECTION II

LESSON I: What Is Not A Plot

In **Holly Lisle's Create A Plot Clinic**, I point out that the **7 Basic Plots in Literature**, (or the 1, or 3, or 20, or 36, depending on who you ask) are a myth of Mermaid-like proportions.

You need to see this myth live, so go to this link at the Internet Public Library:

http://www.ipl.org/div/farq/plotFARQ.html

Beginners look "7 basic plots" up thinking they'll be able to memorize these puppies and then they'll always know what to write.

When you look at the lists, though, your teeth start to itch.

"[wo]man vs. nature" is not a plot.

"Type A, happy ending" is not a plot. (That's not even a helpful conflict. Foster-Harris manages in the four paragraphs listing his theories to turn writing into a black hole of tedium, sucking the life out of writers looking for help. Read "1 Plot" and "3 Plots" on

21

the **ipl.org** site with your tedium-blocking glasses taped to your face.)

"Escape" is not a plot.

Gimme a break. You sit down at a writers' conference and field questions about your next book, and someone asks "What's your book about?" and you say, "Escape," and then sit back like you said something useful, and every eye in the room is going to glaze over.

Not a single one of these things is a plot.

Excluding Foster-Harris, however, these lists do offer something both wonderful and useful.

They offer conflicts. Conflicts are spectacularly handy in writing a novel. But don't mistake them for plots.

What is a plot?

DEFINITION: *PLOT is the series of events that move the characters and story forward.*

Memorize that definition. It will save you a world of pain when you're trying to put a plot together.

Your plot will consist of characters struggling with conflicts toward a goal, whether known or unknown to them. Plot has a beginning, a middle, and an end.

Plot Does Things.

Your Turn

- **Memorize the definition of PLOT.**

- Walk around the house (or work) repeating the words, **"Plot is not conflict,"** until you either can do this in your sleep, or until someone threatens to haul you away and lock you in a padded room.

- **Familiarize yourself with the various** *conflicts* that are listed as plots, at:

  ## http://www.ipl.org/div/farq/plotFARQ.html

In **Lesson Two**, you'll start building your own plot outline using the Mix 'N Match Conflicts technique.

This second lesson picks up where the first one left off. You'll be choosing conflicts and beginning to develop them into the seeds for your plot.

LESSON II: Mix 'N Match Conflict

In your first lesson, you determined that the mythical **7 Basic Plots** and their ilk do not meet the test for plots.

That is, **they are not a series of events that move the characters and story forward.**

But they're not useless.

You're going to use these lists to start building a plot, coming up with ideas to create a story from scratch.

Here's how it'll work. I'll do a demo, giving you such tools as you need do the exercise. Then you'll do the exercise.

For these lessons, start out fresh, with no idea and no preconceptions of where you're going or what you'll get. You need to discover how simple this process really is.

Ready?

You don't know your characters, you don't know your world, you don't, in fact, know anything but that you want to write a story.

So let's scroll down the list of conflicts on the **Internet Public Library** page:

http://www.ipl.org/div/farq/plotFARQ.html

and randomly pick three conflicts (avoiding anything that says Foster-Harris on it for fear of your story catching something nasty).

I'll Start

I've closed my eyes and pointed, and come up with:

- [wo]man vs. the supernatural
- Rivalry
- Adultery

Yuck. I hate adultery stories, but there has to be some way to make this cool.

I'll choose the **Cliffhanger** structure (**Plot Clinic**, p.31) because I love potboilers. They're fun to write.

And I'll use **Tool 1: Question** (**Plot Clinic** p.41) to throw four questions at this mess.

- What is the supernatural challenge the main character faces?

- Who is the main character's rival, and why?

- Who committed adultery, and why?
- How does adultery tie into the supernatural element?

With question four, I just realized that I already did one book with exactly these elements in **Night Echoes**, so I'm going to have to fight to keep from going down the same road. I could just change the conflicts I picked at random to new ones, but where would the challenge be with that?

Your Turn

Get out your EXERCISE SIX (Lesson 2) worksheet.

- Sit down with the Internet Public Library's list of conflicts, and **pick any three conflicts**.

- **Choose a story structure**, so that you'll know how the book is going to go together and what elements you need. (Use the **Create A Plot Clinic** for help, or pick cliffhanger if you aren't familiar with other structures. I'll walk you through the cliffhanger structure as we go.)

- Ask four questions about the three conflicts you've chosen that will help tie them together. Good questions include the words who, what, when, where, why, and how, and cannot be answered with a Yes or a No.

In **Lesson Three**, you'll go answer those questions, and start building your plot.

You'll dip briefly into character before answering your plotting questions in this lesson.

LESSON III: Questions and Answers

To quickly recap from Lesson Two, my conflicts were:

- [wo]man vs. the supernatural
- Rivalry
- Adultery

My structure was **Cliffhanger**.

And my questions were:

- What is the supernatural challenge the main character faces?
- Who is the main character's rival, and why?
- Who committed adultery, and why?
- How does adultery tie into the supernatural element?

At this point, I'm going to have to commit a bit of effort to my character, about whom I still know nothing.

I'll Start

Using **Holly Lisle's Create A Character Clinic** and massively abbreviating for space, I'll use just one of the seven critical facets of human character. More importantly, I'm not going to choose an obvious one that seems to be ready-made for this story. Instead, I'm going to pick **Work & Play**.

And I'm going to ask two questions specifically to develop her character:

What is the character's play?
What price does she pay to pursue her private interests?

I'll answer my first character question first.

- **What is the character's play?**

The character's hobby and passion, I decide, is downhill skiing, and she works like a dog during the week, picking up extra hours whenever she can, to pay for her annual month-long trip to one of the world's top ski resorts--a different one each year.

(Why downhill skiing? I have no clue. It's what popped into my mind, so I'm running with it. I've done a little of it, it's fun, and it's a fine way to get yourself in serious trouble in the blink of an eye.)

So.

Now, knowing at least a little something about my main character, I can go back to my plot questions. I don't have to answer these in any particular order...and I don't. I go to this question next.

- **Who is the main character's rival, and why?**

This one is the quickest to answer. I can figure the rival can be another skier, someone with whom Mica (I don't know why I chose that name, it was just there) has crossed paths over the years. Perhaps someone she was once great friends with. Ex-friends do make the most unnerving enemies.

And, ah, the adultery.

Let's say that the enmity between them is deserved.

- **Who committed adultery, and why?**

Let's say that Mica bedded the ex-friend's husband, and got caught. That's a really good reason to hate someone. Let's also say that the ex-friend (Sonja) lost her husband over the whole ordeal.

But wait.

I'm going to pull out my other two questions:

- **What is the supernatural challenge the main character faces?**

And:

- **How does adultery tie into the supernatural element?**

Let's REALLY run this puppy through a wringer.

Let's say Sonja paid the ultimate price for Mica's infidelity. On a trip where Mica, her boyfriend, Sonja and her husband went skiing together, Sonja's husband was supposed to meet Sonja on one of the black diamond slopes for a late afternoon run. He didn't show up, so Sonja ran the slope alone, fell and broke her leg, and in an ensuing blizzard died of exposure because no one was there to help her.

Sonja is now haunting Mica. The cheating husband is long gone, the nameless boyfriend is long gone, and Mica has avoided the ski slopes for the past three years, driven to the edge of sanity by her guilt and Sonja's ghost.

This year, she's going to return to the slope where Sonja died and attempt to make amends with the ghost by running the black-diamond slope alone.

And I'm well on my way to writing my cliffhanger-structured novel, **Haunted Hills** (terrible title, isn't it?), which will have some real cliffs over which poor Mica can hang.

Finally, I'll give myself a tentative ending. Sonja's ghost will be banished to the netherworlds from whence she came, Mica, having suffered for cheating with her best friend's husband, will be suitably punished and suitably repentant, or in one of those grim twisty novels, Mica herself will end up dead.

Anyway, your turn.

Your Turn

Get out your EXERCISE SEVEN (Lesson 3) worksheet.

- Briefly figure out who your character is, what matters to him or her, and why.

- Start connecting what you know about your character with the questions you've asked about your conflict.

- Trust your subconscious mind to feed you cool suggestions, let odd, unplanned connections form, and follow where they lead. (None of what I did above was planned ahead of time. I am building this as I write the lessons.)

- Save yourself time and headaches by figuring out a possible ending for your story (use **Section I** to do this).

In **Lesson Four**, you'll start creating candy bar scenes.

Holly Lisle

*Last time, you did a microscopic bit of work on your characters using only ONE of the seven critical areas of character development and a mere two questions from **Holly Lisle's Create A Character Clinic**, and you used your four conflict questions and that one aspect of character to create the beginning threads of your plot.*

If you did the exercises, you also have an ending, however rudimentary.

So now it's time for...

LESSON IV: Candy Bar Scenes

Now you're going to have what is probably the most fun in the whole plotting process. You're going to sketch out candy bar scenes.

A candy bar scene is a big scene you just can't wait to write. Your opening scene, your epic struggle, and your big finale are all candy bar scenes, but you can have as many as you like. You can make the whole book nothing but candy bars and transitions, if you want. I've certainly done it a few times. Such books are a blast to write. An example of a book that was all candy bar scenes is **Sympathy for the Devil**, the story of an RN who bargained with God to have mercy on the souls in hell, and who failed to figure God's sense of humor into her bargaining. That novel is available online where you got *this* book.

For this lesson, you're going to trot back to the Internet Public Library for their nifty list of misnamed conflicts:

http://www.ipl.org/div/farq/plotFARQ.html

Select FIVE conflicts. I'll show you what to do with them.

I'll Start

Boy, closing my eyes is being really cruel to me.

I got:

- Murderous Adultery

- Discovery of the Dishonor of a Loved One

- Wretched Excess

- Supplication (in which the Supplicant must beg something from Power in authority)

- Enmity of Kinsmen

On first glance, this doesn't seem like a particularly promising list. It seems redundant in parts and unrelated in other parts. But it does offer me one interesting opening, and I'll go for that. **Enmity of Kinsmen** seems pretty promising.

I'll consider that my protagonist, Mica, has somehow been blamed for her best friend's death by the best friend's husband. Maybe blaming her was his way of transferring guilt.

Maybe he's been spying on her for the last three years, and on discovering Mica was returning to the scene of their liaison and Sonja's death, has gone just a bit over the deep end.

I can envision an exciting scene in which the widowed husband sabotages Mica's skis in order to murder her without getting caught (hey, there's Murderous Adultery, too).

I can see in my mind's eye another scene where she flees onto the mountain and he hunts her with a rifle.

Wretched Excess seems pretty promising, too.

Maybe the widowed husband is rich, or at least well off. Maybe he's staying at the lodge and burying himself in wine, women, and song. Mica could run into him while he's hot-tubbing with a bunch of snow bunnies, and not realize her danger because he's very drunk at the time.

Discovery of the Dishonor of a Loved One seems kind of old hat. We already know about Mica and Sonja's adulterous spouse.

But wait.

What about Sonja, the ghost? Why did she go out on that black diamond slope alone?

Scene in which the reader discovers that Sonja, far from being innocent, had made a deal with her husband to seduce Mica in order to blackmail her—and meantime, was having affairs with other men to blackmail them.

Hmm. This suddenly casts a different light on the widowed husband and his vengeance quest. Maybe HE was the innocent, and Sonja and Mica were working in tandem. Maybe HE and Mica were both uninvolved in Sonja's scheme, but he doesn't know about how Sonja was using him and blames Mica.

And **Supplication**. Hmm. That one seems kind of obvious.

Killer husband corners ex-fling, rifle in hand, and Mica begs for her life, not just to Sonja's widowed husband, but also to Sonja herself.

Now, as my last order of business for this lesson (and in order to be able to use these things), I need to turn each candy bar scene into a single, concise sentence:

Sonja's widowed husband Sam sabotages Mica's skis in order to murder her without getting caught

Sam hunts Mica with a sniper rifle as she flees up the mountain toward wilderness.

Mica discovers Sam, Sonja's widowed husband, stalking her because he knows she's coming, is staying at the same resort she's at when into him while he's hot-tubbing with a bunch of snow bunnies.

Mica receives a video (or videos) of Sonja with important married men, and a tape of her discussing her blackmail source of income with an unknown party.

Sam, Sonja's widowed husband, corners Mica and prepares to kill her, and and Mica begs for her life, not just to Sonja's widowed husband, but also to Sonja herself.

Over to you.

Your Turn

Get out your EXERCISE EIGHT (Lesson 4) worksheet.

Write out at least five candy bar scenes using the Internet Public Library list for seed ideas. Introduce new conflicts and figure out how to link them to the old conflicts.

Continue working out candy bar scenes until you have fifteen or twenty.

In **Lesson Five**, you'll be ordering your scenes for maximum conflict.

Last time, you created a handful or three of candy-bar scenes.

This time, you're going to put them in a couple of different orders in order to create different effects for your novel. Again, I'll demonstrate, and then you'll do your own list ordering.

LESSON V: Ordering Scenes for Conflict

Here are my candy bar scenes. In order to keep this short, I'm only organizing the ones I created last time, plus a handful of others that have occurred to me in the interim. You'll have a lot more, so the effects you'll get from reordering your scenes will be a lot more impressive.

Sonja's widowed husband Sam sabotages Mica's skis in order to murder her without getting caught

Sam hunts Mica with a sniper rifle as she flees up the mountain toward wilderness.

Mica discovers Sam, Sonja's widowed husband, is staying at the same resort she's at when into him while he's hot-tubbing with a bunch of snow bunnies. He doesn't see her, so she thinks he doesn't know she's there. She doesn't know he's her stalker.

Mica receives a video (or videos) of Sonja with important married men, and a tape of her discussing her blackmail source of income with an unknown party.

Sam, Sonja's widowed husband, corners Mica and prepares to kill her, and and Mica begs for her life, not just to Sonja's widowed husband, but also to Sonja herself.

Mica realizes Sonja was murdered.

A masked man shoots Sam, and Sam dies.

The masked man, whom we hoped was a good guy, goes after her to kill her.

Mica makes daring, mind-boggling escape, and we think she's free.

Would-be killer corners Mica for one final go, and they fight.

Mica triumphs.

Mica arrives at the ski resort.

In a confrontation with an employee, we discover why Mica is at the ski resort.

Remember, I'm using a **cliffhanger** structure, which means the majority of my scenes, and ALL of my big candy bar scenes, are going to end with somebody clinging to life by fingernails, or with something exciting unfinished.

I'll Start

TAKE ONE

First I'll arrange the plot in linear order.

- Mica arrives at the ski resort.

- In a confrontation with an employee, we discover why Mica is at the ski resort.

- Mica discovers Sam, Sonja's widowed husband, is staying at the same resort she's at when she spots him hot-tubbing with a bunch of snow bunnies. He doesn't see her, so she thinks he doesn't know she's there. She doesn't know he's her stalker.

- Mica receives a video (or videos) of Sonja with important married men, and a tape of her discussing her blackmail source of income with an unknown party.

- Sonja's widowed husband Sam sabotages Mica's skis in order to murder her without getting caught

- Mica realizes Sonja was murdered.

- Sam hunts Mica with a sniper rifle as she flees up the mountain toward wilderness.

- Sam, Sonja's widowed husband, corners Mica and prepares to kill her, and and Mica begs for her life, not just to Sonja's widowed husband, but also to Sonja herself.

- A masked man shoots Sam, and Sam dies.

- The masked man, whom we hoped was a good guy, goes after her to kill her.

- Mica makes daring, mind-boggling escape, and we think she's free.

- Would-be killer corners Mica for one final go, and they fight.

- Mica triumphs.

This is as straightforward as storytelling gets. You're working to a strict timeline, and you simply write each event in the order in which it happens. It works, and it will get the job done.

But it's not your only alternative, nor is it always your best.

TAKE TWO

Now, I'll pull a Joss Whedon on this (From the episode *Out Of Gas*, **Firefly**) and run it in almost reverse, all except for the ending.

- Would-be killer corners Mica for one final go, and they fight. (We wonder what caused this).

- Mica makes daring, mind-boggling escape, and we think she's free. (We discover what caused the fight in the previous scene, but now wonder why he was after her.)

- The masked man, whom we hoped was a good guy, goes after her to kill her. (We discover that Mica initially mistook her would-be killer for a friend and rescuer. Why?)

- A masked man shoots Sam, and Sam dies. (We discover WHY Mica trusted the man initially, but now we wonder why the first guy was trying to kill her. Who IS she, what does she know?)

- Sam, Sonja's widowed husband, corners Mica and prepares to kill her, and and Mica begs for her life, not just to Sonja's widowed husband, but also to Sonja herself. (Now we find out that he believes Mica was in league with Sonja against him. But who's Sonja?)

- Sam hunts Mica with a sniper rifle as she flees up the mountain toward wilderness. (We see where the trouble got ugly)

- Mica realizes Sonja was murdered. (And here we wonder which of the two killers we've met killed her.)

- Sonja's widowed husband Sam sabotages Mica's skis in order to murder her without getting caught (We see a planned ski accident, and suspect Sam as Sonja's killer, too.)

- Mica receives a video (or videos) of Sonja with important married men, and a tape of her discussing her blackmail source of income with an unknown party. (Here we find out about Sonja, and discover she was not a good person.)

- Mica discovers Sam, Sonja's widowed husband, is staying at the same resort she's at when she spots him hot-tubbing with a bunch of snow bunnies. He doesn't see her, so she thinks he doesn't know she's there. She doesn't know he's her stalker. (Here we still suspect Sam as Sonja's killer. He doesn't seem too broken up.)

- In a confrontation with an employee, we discover why Mica is at the ski resort.

- A major flashback, to when Sam and Sonja and Mica and her boyfriend are laughing and having a wonderful time at the resort, before everything went bad. (This is an alternate scene, in which we now identify the masked killer as Mica's ex boyfriend, and recognize his voice from the tapes, and realize that HE was working as Sonja's blackmail partner.

- Mica triumphs. (Finally, we find out that Mica, badly injured and possibly dead along with her would-be killer in the first scene, lives.)

You can see where this notches up the tension quite a bit...you're constantly pushing the reader to ask "Why are they here?" and "How did this happen?" and you're answering that question for the reader at the same time that you're presenting a new one.

It's a pretty neat structure if you don't run to long with it. Great, in other words, for short stories, TV episodes, stage plays, shorter movies—like that.

NOT good for novels. You don't want your readers banding together and hiring a hit man to get you for stressing them out.

Your Turn

Get out your EXERCISE NINE (Lesson 5) worksheet.

There are a million other ways to order your scenes. Don't do a million. Just do a few. (If you do these on index cards, you can mix them around much more easily than on a computer or with paper.)

Do a linear order first, just to get the story into your head.

Then experiment with reversing the order, with using lesser flashbacks and flashforwards, and with playing with your suspense in order to keep your plot fascinating and your readers hooked. You'll find the how-to's for all of this in detail in **Holly Lisle's Create A Plot Clinic**.

Always look at the way the story would be affected if you told it in a different order than the obvious linear one. Use the worksheets to figure out where to keep your suspense and what to emphasize.

That's it for this time.

In **Lesson Six**, you'll learn to fill in the bare spaces in your plot with good stuff, not padding.

You're pretty close to having a workable plot outline. This lesson will show you how to fill in the blanks--the areas where candy bars haven't been, and where you have big gaps between your action.

LESSON VI: Filling In The Blanks

I'm going to take two of my scenes from the previous outline that had a big gap in the action between them, and show you one way to fill in with good, high-quality, conflict-filled scenes.

(There are nineteen other tools you can use in **Holly Lisle's Create A Plot Clinic.**)

You don't want to pad. You don't want to follow your character through a day of taking a shower, thinking in the shower, drinking tea, thinking while drinking tea, driving to work, thinking while driving to work, sitting at a desk, thinking while ....

You get the picture. This is a fine way to induce coma in your readers. But generally, you want them to survive reading your book...so they can buy the next one, or at least write you a nice letter telling you how much they enjoyed that one.

So.

I'll go first, and walk you through the process. You'll then start adding good scenes in between your blank scenes.

I'll Start

Here are my scenes:

- Mica discovers Sam, Sonja's widowed husband, is staying at the same resort she's at when she spots him hot-tubbing with a bunch of snow bunnies. He doesn't see her, so she thinks he doesn't know she's there. She doesn't know he's her stalker.

- Mica receives a video (or videos) of Sonja with important married men, and a tape of her discussing her blackmail source of income with an unknown party.

Using my Question tool (Plot Clinic, page , I'm going to ask my character questions about those two scenes.

- Mica, what do you think Sam is doing at the ski resort?

- What sort of contact are you having with Sonja's ghost now that you're here? (I forgot about the whole ghost part of the storyline until now, and have realized that I'm going to need to work it into the whole plot.)

- What sort of a reaction are you having to being on a ski slope again after three years, and being back at this particular resort?

- How do you receive the videos and tape of Sonja? Can she be involved it getting them to you, or leading you to them?

Those are all pretty good questions, I think. We hit inner conflict with Mica's reaction to Sam and Mica's reaction to the ski resort, and we hit external conflict with ghost appearances and the arrival/discovery of the videos and tape of Sonja.

In real life, I'd work out all of these questions, and create scenes for all of them, but for this exercise, I'll just do one---Question 2.

I'll let my mind ramble here, talking to myself through the keyboard with the issue of Mica and Sonja's ghost.

It would be too cliché to have Mica staying in the same room she was in before, and a bit too pat.

It would be just flat hokey to have her staying in the room (or cabin .... would having her rent a cabin be more fun?) ...

Okay.

Stop.

If both couples *were staying in one of those pricey cabins at the resort when Sonja died (having gone in on it together), it would suddenly make sense if Mica stayed in the same place.*

There's a sense of pilgrimage, then, rather than the anonymity of a hotel room.

It would provide a connection with the way she locates hidden videos.

It would make haunting by Sonja a bit more practical, since there would be a previous tie to the place.

51

And it would make isolating Mica as things go bad very easy, and very scary.

So that's what I'll do. This just became a quick lesson in staying flexible with your plot, too. **(Bonus points!)**

So. Interesting scenes I get include:

- Mica walks through the cabin and comes face to face with Sonja's ghost, who tries to force her to the balcony (I'm thinking the videos could be hidden in a package beneath the balcony, or in it if it's constructed correctly...

- Mica resolves to stay away from the main resort in order to avoid Sam, but Sam pays her a friendly visit that is terribly awkward.

That's two scenes from one question, and you can see where you could get a lot more.

Your Turn

Get out your EXERCISE TEN (Lesson 6) worksheet.

Select two scenes in your plot outline that have a significant gap between them.

Ask your main character questions about those two scenes, how he reacts to them, what he's doing in between them, and so on. Focus on CONFLICT, on things that go wrong, that create tension, that leave the reader wondering What Happens Next.

Use the answers you get from these questions to create new scenes. Make sure each scene contains conflict.

You've built a workable plot outline now, using basic conflicts you can find at the Internet Public Library:

www.ipl.org/div/farq/plotFARQ.html

Now it's time to write the book.

LESSON VII: Plotting As You Go

As you write, you'll probably find, as many a dismayed general has discovered, that no battle plan survives first contact with the enemy. As you get into your book, you're going to have to adapt, change things, discard characters and storylines that don't work, add in new things that do.

This final plotting lesson will offer one method to help you figure your way through the changes that come up as you're working through your story.

Holly Lisle's Create A Plot Clinic offers specific, detailed instructions, examples, tool tips, and more on:

- rethinking plot points that don't work;

- great ideas that arrive way late in the writing process and would require changes throughout;

- how to change characters;

- how to change worldbuilding;

- how to change your primary conflicts, and how to plot a great ending.

What You Face As Things Change

In this lesson, we're just going to deal with fixing little changes as you write.

Last time, I discovered that my protagonist, Mica, was staying in a private cabin at the ski resort, not the lodge.

This is the sort of change that seems small on the surface, and if you discover it while you're doing your initial plotting, nothing could be easier than fixing it. But if you're already a third of the way through the book, or two thirds of the way through, what do you do?

Do you stick with having her stay in the lodge, knowing that the story would be worlds better if you ran with the idea of isolating her in the cabin?

It's a personal choice, and your deadline and your feelings about rewriting will dictate your choices, but I generally go for the great change that will heighten the conflicts.

My process for changing a major element in the middle of writing the book is:

- Pretend everything I wrote up to the point of the big change is exactly as it should be.

- Plot out everything that will be different now that I've made the change.

- Write the rest of the book with the new element in place, keeping track of the things that happen because of the change that would not have happened without it.

- Write down each change that is going to need to have something happen earlier in the book in order for that change to occur.

- Go back after I've finished the first draft and write in each incident that created the later changes.

Doing the ending feels a bit scary, like walking on a tightrope without a net. The net is there, though.

It's the revision process, and as long as you understand that the net is there, that **You're Going To Go Back And Fix Everything,** you can prevent yourself from endlessly going back and messing around with the first part of the book, making changes that later prove to be unnecessary.

If you write the first draft all the way to the ending, you'll ONLY make changes to the first part that are relevant.

If you stop midway through and go back and piddle, you're just going to make a mess. Trust me---I've done it both ways a bunch of times, and pretending I got it right the first time has proved over and over again to be the only way to fly.

I'll Start

Let's say that I'm halfway through the book, and I've written a number of scenes that reference Mica in her room in the lodge, and show her hanging out in the public spaces there. Halfway through, when I discover my great idea (to put her in an isolated cabin), I tell myself I never wrote those scenes---that instead I wrote great paranoid isolated scenes with her alone in the cabin, haunted by the ghost of her dead friend and by her own guilt.

I write a scene that, for it to work, requires that she has to have been in her cabin at a certain time on a certain day doing something that Sam could see through a window. So I write a plot card (**Plot Clinic**) for the scene that I should have written, and stick it in with my other plot cards.

It says something like:

REWRITE OR DO NEW SCENE

Mica in the kitchen chopping vegetables for stew with a big knife (give knife subtle emphasis because it's going to be weapon of self defense later.)

Note: Sam is watching from outside--consider cut scene from his point of view.

I'll do one of these for each situation where something has to have happened earlier in the book, but hasn't.

When I'm done, I'll put all the scenes into a workable order, and do my revision.

Your Turn

Keep this lesson handy. When you need it, remember your five steps:

- Pretend you got everything up to the point of your change right the first time. Keep writing new material.

- Do new plot cards as necessary for the parts of the book you have not yet written.

- Write the rest of the book with the new element in place, keeping track of the things that happen because of the change that would not have happened without it.

- Do a new plot card for everything that you're going to have to go back and fix.

- Fix everything in the revision, not before you have the first draft done.

This brings your course on **Using Basic Conflicts to Build Plot** to an end.

Good luck with your story. Write with joy.

Holly

About the Author

Holly Lisle is the author of more than thirty published novels (and counting), including the recent re-release of her award-winning first novel, **Fire in the Mist**, and her upcoming re-release of **Cadence Drake: Hunting The Corrigan's Blood**, which will kick off the ten-book Cadence Drake series.

Holly had an ideal childhood for a writer…which is to say, it was filled with foreign countries and exotic terrains, alien cultures, new languages, the occasional earthquake, flood, or civil war, and one story about a bear, which follows:

"So. Back when I was ten years old, my father and I had finished hunting ducks for our dinner and were walking across the tundra in Alaska toward the spot on the river where we'd tied our boat. We had a couple miles to go by boat to get back to the Moravian Children's Home, where we lived.

"My father was carrying the big bag of decoys and the shotgun; I was carrying the small bag of ducks.

"It was getting dark, we could hear the thud, thud, thud of the generator across the tundra, and suddenly he stopped, pointed down to a pie-pan sized indentation in the tundra that was rapidly filling with water, and said, in a calm and steady voice, "That's a bear footprint. From the size of it, it's a grizzly. The fact that the track is filling with water right now means the bear's still around."

"Which got my attention, but not as much as what he said next.
" 'I don't have the gun with me that will kill a bear,' he told me. 'I just have the one that will make him angry. So if we see the bear, I'm going to shoot him so he'll attack me. I want you to drop what you're carrying, run to the river, follow it to the boat, get the boat back home, and tell everyone what happened.'

"The rest of our walk was very quiet. He was, I'm sure, listening for the bear. I was doing my damnedest to make sure that I remembered where the boat was, how to get to it, how to start the pull-cord engine, and how to drive it back home in the dark down the Kwethluk River's looping, slough-crossed course, because I did not want to let him down.

"We were not eaten by a bear that night…but neither is that walk back from our hunt for supper a part of my life I'll ever forget.
"I keep that story in mind as I write. If what I'm putting on paper isn't at least as memorable as having a grizzly stalking my father and me across the tundra following us and our bag of delicious-smelling ducks, it doesn't make my cut."

You can find her, her novels, her writing courses, 100,000 words of free writing articles and workshops, her weblog, and more at:

http://HollyLisle.com

My Writing Courses

I offer both short, specific courses about specific areas of writing fiction, for example, plot, character creation, worldbuilding, writing scenes, and so on.

I also offer three multi-lesson courses for writers who are serious about publishing your work:

- **How to Think Sideways**: Career Survival School for Writers
- **How to Revise Your Novel**: How to Get the Book You WANT from the Wreck you Wrote.
- **How to Write a Series**: Master the Art of Episodic Fiction

Not all courses may be available at all times. You can always find what I'm currently offering here:

http://howtothinksideways.com/writing-courses

My Novels, Short Stories, and More

I've written a lot of books in a number of genres: science fiction, fantasy, young adult, suspense, and "defies classification."

I've reissued a number of my books that were out of print for years, and am writing and publishing new work currently.

To find my currently available works, go here:

http://hollylisle.com/new-works-and-reprints

And to get news on when I have a new novel or collection coming out, sign up here:

http://hollylisle.com/the-fun-with-teeth-sign-up-page